DMN Pocket Reference

A Practical Reference Guide to
the Decision Model and Notation
Specification version 1.1

Kenneth J Sherry

First Published 2018
By Admaks Publishing
www.admaks.com

First edition 2018

About The Book

The DMN Pocket Reference is a guide for users of DMN (Decision Model and Notation 1.1.).

The DMN Pocket Reference provides in-depth explanations of the DMN elements using easily comprehensible diagrams.

The DMN Pocket Reference defines the DMN elements contained in a decision model diagram as described in the Object Management Group (OMG) specification.

The notations are clearly portrayed using graphical diagrams showing how they are depicted, each with a brief description.

Examples have been included to demonstrate the use and implementation of the DMN notations.

The DMN Pocket Reference also illustrates the link between DMN, Decision Logic and BPMN.

This book is intended for readers how have knowledge of BPMN (Business Process Model and Notation) and an understanding of business process modelling.

For information on BPMN the author has published the following two books:

Business Process Modelling with BPMN

-   *ISBN 9781479118052*

This is a course book designed for newcomers to business process modelling.

Complete BPMN Pocket Reference

-   *ISBN 9781507546475*

A practical user reference guide to the complete BPMN specification version 2.02.

Table of Contents

Introduction

DMN is designed to expand and detail the specific decision-making tasks required in business process design, making the decisions legible for the business stakeholders.

Utilising BPMN and DMN together there are three different perspectives to Decision Management Design, which allows for a more detailed overview.

1. BPMN which uses existing modelling standards, describes the coordination of decision-making within business processes by defining specific tasks or activities.

2. DMN which provides two further perspectives to Decision Management Design.

   a) Decision Requirements Diagrams (DRD) define the decisions made in BPMN tasks, interrelationships, the input information and the requirements for decision logic.

   b) Decision Logic Models define the decisions in sufficient detail to allow validation and/or automation.

Decision Requirements Diagrams and Decision Logic Models together complete the decision model called a Decision Requirements Graph (DRG).

The DRG complements a business process model by specifying in detail the decision making carried out by the process tasks.

DRD Notations

DMN provides specific notations for decision requirements modelling, in order to produce a Decision Requirements Diagram (DRD).

There are five different DRD notations:

1. Input Data
2. Decision
3. Listed Input Data
4. Business Knowledge Model
5. Knowledge Source

Simply put

- The Input Data notation is equivalent to the **BPMN Data Input Object**
- The Decision notation is equivalent to the **BPMN Business Rules Task,** requiring an input to produce an output
- Listed Input Data notation is depicted together with the Decision notation
- The Business Knowledge Model notation depicts the rules logic for the specific decision step, in a business process flow
- The Knowledge Source notation depicts the source of the knowledge required and obtained, specifically to be used by Business Knowledge Model notations and/or Decision notations

Input Data Notation

An Input Data notation is shown with two parallel straight sides and two semi-circular ends, drawn with a solid line.

The Input Data notation represents the active information provided by the business process requirements.

The Input Data label should have the same name as the **BPMN Data Object** and be clearly displayed to prevent confusion.

If more than one Input Data notation is used in a DRD, the unique name of each element should reflect the actual business process data used in the decision making.

Note

Input Data can be anything that is regarded as a data element i.e. letter, paper invoice, email, excel, word documents or database files etc.

Decision Notation

Decision

A Decision notation is shown as a rectangle, drawn with solid lines.

A Decision notation represents the decision logic output produced from a number of inputs, which may be referenced by one or more Business Knowledge Model notations.

Note

The Input Data notation depicts active business process information, whereas the Business Knowlege Model notation is static information and is used to evaluate the decision logic results.

Listed Input Data Notation

Decision
Data Input 1 Data Input 2

The Input Data labels are listed directly on the Decision notation, separated by a horizontal line.

The Listed Input Data notation is an alternative way to display requirements for input data.

This is especially useful when DRDs are large or complex.

Business Knowledge Model Notation

A Business Knowledge Model notation is shown as a rectangle with two clipped corners, drawn with a solid line

A Business Knowledge Model notation represents the static information used to determine the decision result of the business process input data.

The Business Knowledge Model notation denotes a function which concentrates business knowledge for a process decision, e.g. business rules, a decision table or an analytic model.

Note

Depending on user requirements and methodology, it is not necessary to include all decision logic in a Business Knowledge Model.

Knowledge Source Notation

A Knowledge Source notation is shown with three straight sides in the form of a rectangle with a wavy line at the bottom.

The Knowledge Source notation represents the information derived from an authoritative source.

Note

The Knowledge Source might be a company policy, the company warrantee Terms and Conditions or the company procurement policy etc.

The Knowledge Source could also be a specific person or management level or a team responsible for defining some decision logic.

NOTES

DRD Requirements Notations

A Decision Requirements Diagram (DRD) allows for three types of connection notations

1. Information Requirement
2. Knowledge Requirement
3. Authority Requirement

Simply put

- The Information Requirement notation is used to show the direction and the connection of the input data from the active information used in decision making

- The Knowledge Requirement notation is used to show from where the specific static business knowledge is derived and used in decision making

- The Authority Requirement notation is used to show the source of the business knowledge

Information Requirement Notation

An Information Requirement notation is represented by a solid line with a solid arrowhead at one end.

The arrow is drawn in the direction of the information flow i.e. towards the notation that requires the information.

The Information Requirement notation indicates where the input data source is derived from.

This notation is used to represent active input decision data.

Note

The Information Requirement notation can be used to show the output of a decision notation used as an input to another notation.

Knowledge Requirement Notation

$- - -$ Knowledge $- - \rightarrow$
        Requirement

A Knowledge Requirement notation is represented by a dashed line and an open arrowhead at one end.

The arrow is drawn in the direction of the information flow i.e. towards a Decision notation.

Knowledge Requirement notations represent the static knowledge necessary for decision making.

Note

Knowledge Requirement notations are drawn between Business Knowledge Model and Decision notations.

Knowledge Requirement notations can be drawn from one Business Knowledge Model notation to another Business Knowledge Model notation.

Authority Requirement Notation

— — — Authority — — ●
Requirement

An Authority Requirement notation is represented by a dashed line with a solid dot at one end.

The Authority Requirement notation denotes the source of knowledge for another DRD notation.

Note

An Authority Requirement notation may be used to show information input to a Knowledge Source Model notation.

Authority Requirement notations can be used to show, for analytical purposes, the information flow from an Input Data notation and/or a Decision notation to a Knowledge Source notation.

DRD Requirements Connections Overview

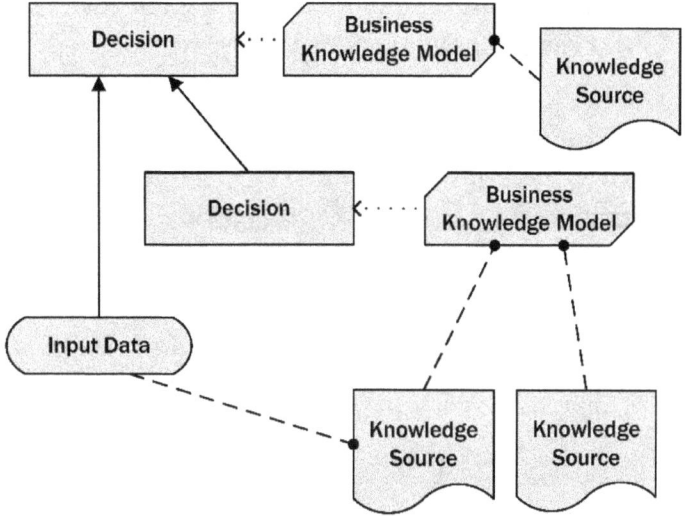

Figure 1: DRD requirements connections overview

Figure1 depicts how the DRD requirements notations can be connected

- Input Data connected to a decision - Information Requirement
- Input Data connected to a knowledge source - Authority Requirement
- Two knowledge Sources connected to a Business Knowledge Model - Authority Requirement
- Decision connected to a Decision - Information Requirement

- A Knowledge Source connected to a Business Knowledge Model - Authority Requirement
- Business Knowledge Model connected to a Decision - Knowledge Requirement

DRD Artefact Notations

The DMN specification only describes three types of artefact notations.

- Group
- Text Annotation
- Association

Group Notation

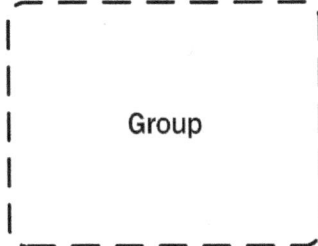

A Group notation is represented by a rounded corner rectangle drawn with a dashed line.

A Group notation is used for documentation or analytic purposes only.

Note

A Group notation can be used to describe groups of notations: decision, business knowledge model, knowledge source and input data, which are part of the same scenario.

Text Annotation Notation

Text

Annotation

A Text Annotation notation is represented by a three-sided partial box, containing the description.

A Text Annotation notation is a mechanism for modellers to provide additional text information for the reader of a DRD and is used to describe various parts of the diagram.

A DRD may contain any number of Text Annotation artefacts.

Association Notation

· · · · · · · · · · ·Association· · · · · · · · · ·

An Association notation is depicted by a dotted line.

An Association notation is used in conjunction with a Text Annotation connected to a DRD notation.

Note
Additional non-standard artefact notations can be included in a DRD.

Modelling a DRD

A DRD allows the modeller to depict the interface between business process models and decision logic models in a graphic form.

A DRD is used to show the different sources of information, where the information is derived from and the specific connections for making business process decisions.

Simple DRD

Figure 2 shows the basic modelling techniques and configurations using DMN notations.

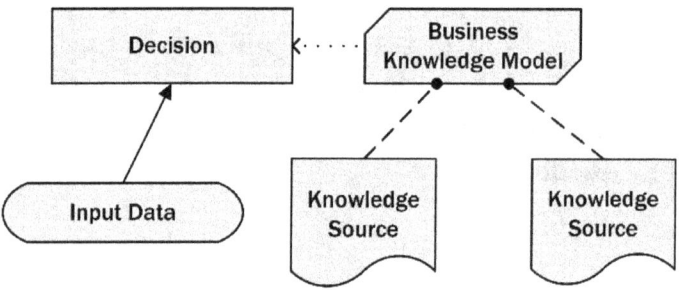

Figure 2: Simple DRD

In figure 2 the Decision notation is used to represent an output determined from a number of inputs using decision logic, which may reference Business Knowledge Models, Knowledge Sources and Input Data.

The Input Data notation denotes information used as the input.

The Input Data notation depicts the active information provided by a Business Process Model.

The Business Knowledge Model notation represents the required business knowledge for the specific decision process sequence task e.g. business rules, a decision table, an analytic model etc.

The Knowledge Source notation represents the information derived from an authoritative source for the Business Knowledge Model.

Two Decision DRD

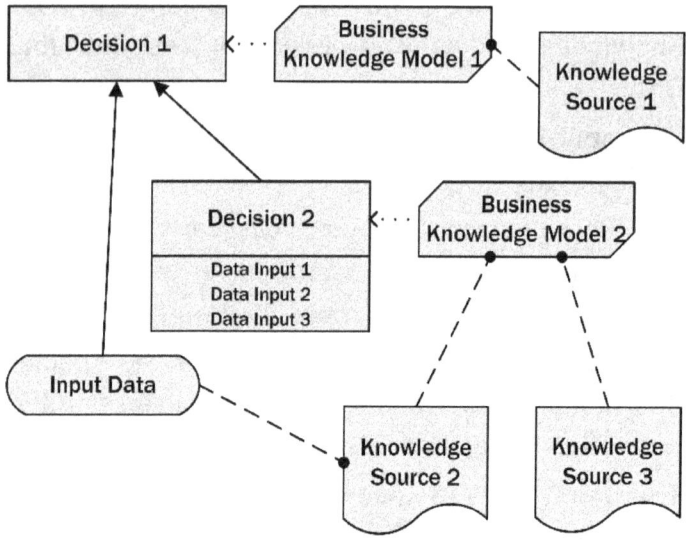

Figure 3: Two decision DRD

Figure 3 includes a second Decision notation (Decision 2) which has been introduced and includes a Listed Data Input notation.

There are three inputs to Decision 1:

1. The output from the Input Data notation
2. The output from Decision 2 notation
3. The output from Business Knowledge Model 1 notation

DMN Pocket Reference

The input to Business Knowledge Model 1 notation is the output from Knowledge Source 1 notation.

There are four inputs to Decision 2:

1. The output from Business Knowledge Model 2 notation
2. The output from the Listed Data Input notation
   - Data input 1
   - Data input 2
   - Data input 3

The Business Knowledge Model 2 notation derives its information from two separate notations

   - Knowledge Source 2
   - Knowledge Source 3

Knowledge Source 2 has a further input from Input Data notation.

Simple DRD Revisited

Figure 4 is a replica of figure 2 however, it shows an example of a business scenario describing the uses of the different notations in a DRD.

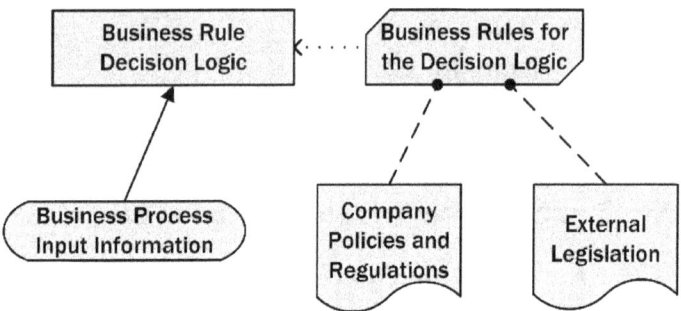

Figure 4: Simple DRD Revisited

In figure 4:

- The process input data information used for decision making is depicted by an Input Data notation (Business Process Input Information)
- The business process decision logic e.g. the program scripts to calculate the result against the business rules is depicted by a Decision notation (Business Rule Decision Logic)
- The business process rules used by the Decision logic is derived from a Business Knowledge Model notation (Business Rules for the Decision Logic)
- The business knowledge business rules for the decision logic is governed by two sources of information:
  a) The company policies and regulations - Knowledge Source notation,
  b) External legislation - Knowledge Source notation,

NOTES

Process Modelling Relationships

DMN is designed to work with BPMN business process models.

There are three different models; Business Process Diagram, Decision Requirements Diagram and Decision Logic Model

- Business Process Diagrams (BPD) depict tasks within business processes where decision-making is required
- Decision Requirements Diagram (DRD) depicts
  a. the decisions in the task
  b. the information requirements
  c. the interrelationship requirements for decision logic
- Decision Logic Model defines the required decisions in sufficient detail to allow validation and/or automation

Note
Used together, the BPD, the DRD and Decision Logic Model provide a complete decision scenario by specifying in detail the decision-making carried out within a decision process task.

Note

Although, DMN and BPMN have a specific relationship, it is not a requirement that DMN be used only in conjunction with BPMN.

DMN can be used autonomously or with other business process modelling techniques.

BPMN Tasks and DMN Decisions

Most BPMN diagrams contain some tasks that involve decision-making which can be modelled in DMN.

These tasks take input data acquired or generated earlier in the process and produce decision outputs which are used later in the process.

Decision outputs may be used in two principal ways

1. They may be used in other process tasks
2. To influence the choice of sequence flows out of a gateway, to determine which sub-processes or tasks are to be executed.

Types of BPMN Tasks Relevant to DMN

BPMN Business Rule Task
A Business Rule Task was defined in BPMN 2 as a placeholder for a business rule decision, which is equivalent to a DMN Decision.

BPMN Service Task
A BPMN Service Task is the equivalent to a DMN Decision Service.

BPMN User Task
A User Task used as a decision and executed as a part of a business process workflow can be defined by a DMN Decision notation.

BPMN Script Task
A Script Task can be used for encoding DMN Decision Logic Models using business process script languages.

BPMN Warranty Check BPD

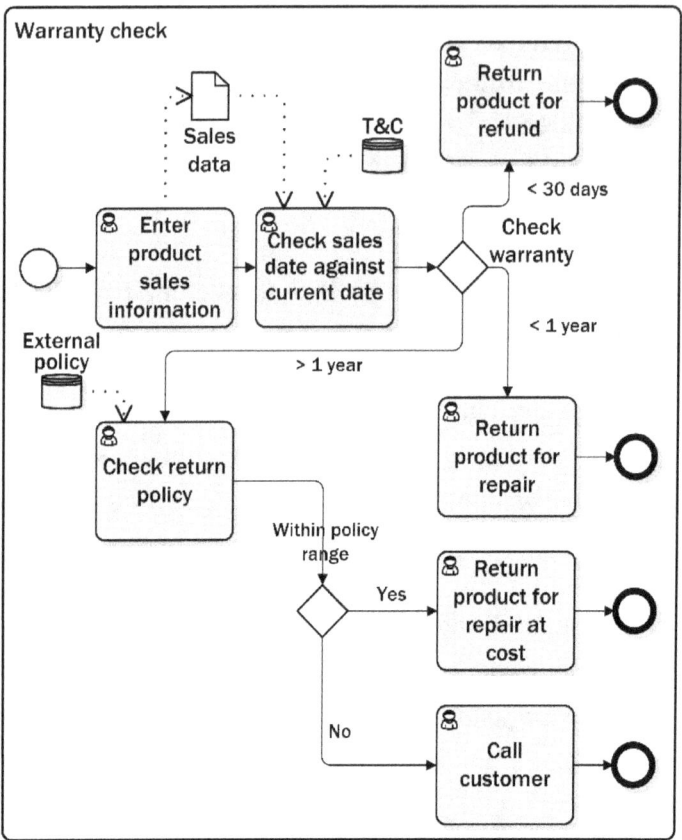

Figure 5: BPMN warranty check BPD

Figure 5 is a basic BPD depicting the process of product return and the warranty decisions.

The product sales information is entered and checked against the sales date and current date to determine the relationship to the business rules.

The business rules are provided by the company T&C to determine whether the product has a valid warranty.

If the product does not have a valid warranty the sales information is checked against an external policy on product returns e.g. a product can be returned for repair within 6 years of purchase at cost to the customer.

The outcome provides the business process task with four different possible outcomes.

- Return product for refund
- Return product for repair
- Return product for repair at cost
- Call customer

BPMN & DMN Relationship Diagram

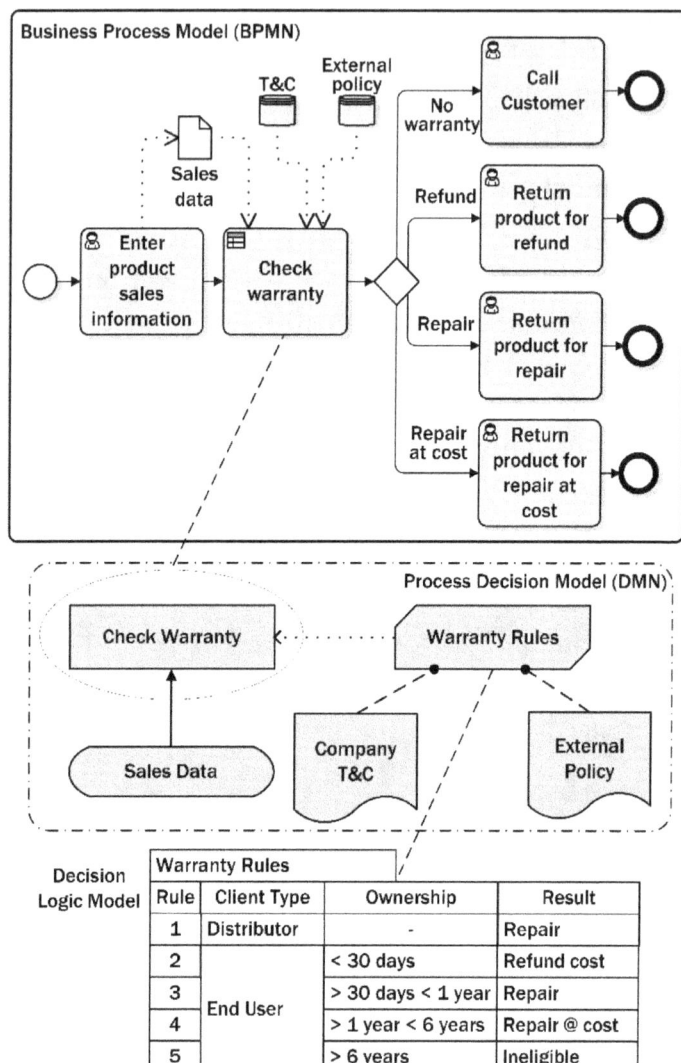

Figure 6: BPMN & DMN Relationship

DMN Pocket Reference

Figure 6 shows a top-down design of a business process model and a process decision model, detailing the role of the business rules and the analytic model.

The diagram is composed of three levels:

- Business Process Model (BPMN) in the form of a Business Process Diagram (BPD)
- Process Decision Model (DMN) in the form of a Decision Requirements Diagram (DRD)
- Decision Logic Model (Business Rules and Analytic Model) in the form of a Decision Table

In figure 6 the Business Process Model (BPMN) shows the business process of a product being returned for refund or repair.

In the Process Decision Model (DMN) the warranty business rules are checked against the sales date and current date to determine the relationship to the business rules.

The input data (Sales Data) to the process decision model is the product sales information provided by the customer.

The information provided to the business knowledge model (Warranty Rules) is
1. Company T&C
2. External Policy on product returns e.g. a product can be returned for repair within 6 years of purchase at a cost to the customer.

The outcome of the business rules logic (Check Warranty) allows the business process tasks to select from different possibilities.

- Call customer
- Return product for refund
- Return product for repair (End user or Distributor)
- Return product for repair at cost

Decision Service

DMN and a Decision Service

A Decision Service isolates the logic behind business decisions, separating it from business processes and the operation application code.

A Decision Service can be either an external or an internal company process.

A Decision Service is a specific automated process decision and has a set of predetermined business rules.

A Decision Service is provided with the input information and responds with a decision outcome.

Note

DMN allows the functionality of a Decision Service to be defined within a decision model but does not specify how the service is created to meet the requirements.

A Decision Service can be designed for internal use or for external access.

The following are some examples of Decision Services

- A credit check where the personal information is supplied to the service and a result is obtained
- A mortgage check where the parameters are supplied and the result provided as an outcome
- A shipment routing service that routes shipments to customers based on demand, contracts and status
- A claims payment service that uses rules to check a claim for authorization to pay while also applying analytics to detect potential fraud

DMN Decision Service Notations

There are two types of decision service notations

- Decision Service
- Divided Decision Service

Simply put

- A Decision Service notation shows a specific automated step in the business process sequence. The output from the decision notation depends on the process input based on the predetermined business rules.

- A Divided Decision Service notation is used when two or more decision services are used in the process sequence in a business process model.

- The input data for a Decision Service notation can come from various sources and can include multiple decision notations.

Note
Decision Service notations use a heavy solid border in much the same way as BPMN call activity notations.

Decision Service Notation

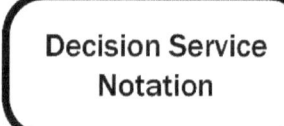

A Decision Service notation is represented as a rectangle with rounded corners, drawn with a heavy solid border.

Decision Service notations should be named and labelled to display other properties i.e. a decision description.

The external decision element is included inside the notation and any inputs are outside the notation.

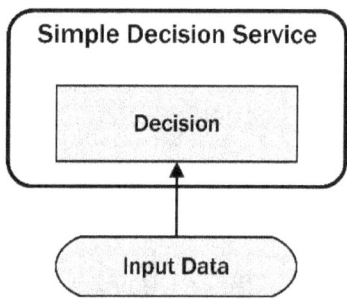

Figure 7: Simple Decision Service

Figure 7 shows a simple decision service notation which requires an input from the process in the form of an Input Data notation.

Decision Service Notation with Decision Input

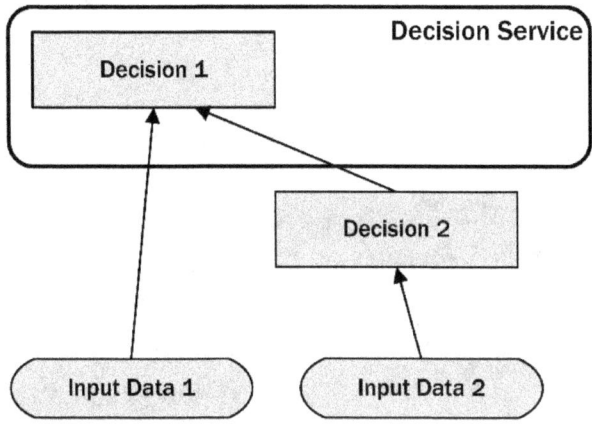

Figure 8: Decision Service with decision input

Figure 8 shows a Decision Service with the following input information

- Input Data 1
- The output from Decision 2 is calculated from Input Data 2

Divided Decision Service Notation

A Divided Decision Service notation is used if the decision requires two or more Decision Services as input to the decision logic.

Divided Decision

Service Notation

A Divided Decision Service notation is represented as a rectangle with rounded corners, divided into two parts by a straight line.

One part of the notation is used only for the output decisions and the label, whereas the other part is used for all the decisions which are not in the set of output decisions.

Either part may include other DMN notations but these will not form part of the definition of the Decision Service.

Note

For clarity, the rectangle or its parts may be shaded, and all the elements comprising of the interface (the output decisions, input decisions and input data) may be drawn with a line that matches the weight and colour of the border.

Divided Decision Service Example

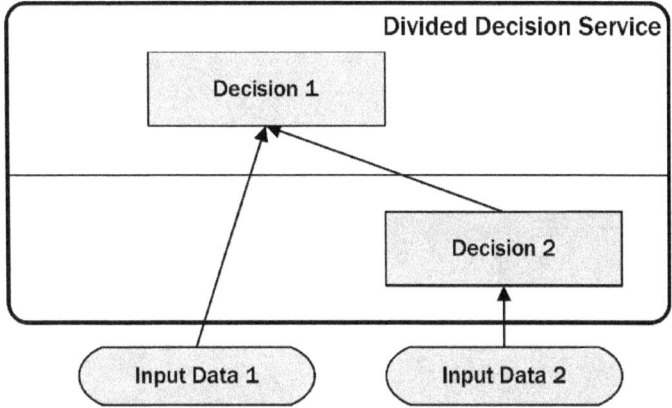

Figure 9: Divided Decision Service

In figure 9:

- Decision 1 and decision 2 are a Decision Service
- Decision 1 requires the input of Decision 2 and Input Data 1
- Decision 2 requires the Input Data 2 to provide an output to Decision 1

Note

Input Data 1 and 2 are external to the Decision Service.

When the Decision Service is called it returns the outcome based on the Input Data and Decisions.

Some information may not be required by the Decision Service as it is already the standard parameter provided.

NOTES

DMN Pocket Reference

Decision Model

Decision Models are a specific area of decision-making for decision requirements and decision logic expressed as a DRD.

Simply put

- A Decision Model depicts the business process decisions as a DRD using DMN notations
- A Decision Model can depict both internal and external decision services
- A Decision Model requires input information which determines the outcomes

Modelling Relationship with a Decision Service

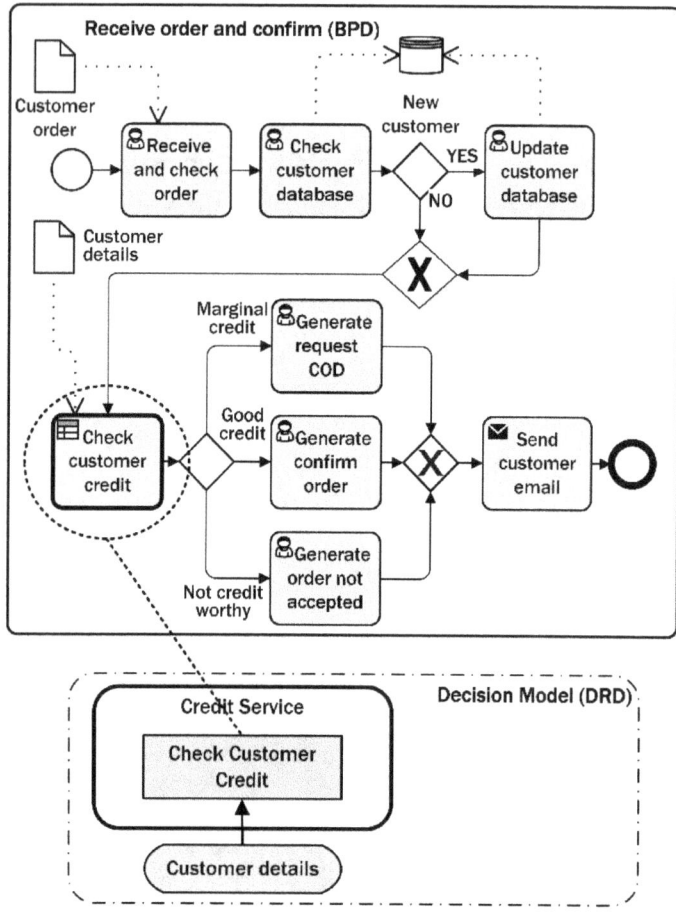

Figure 10: Decision service process modelling relationship

Figure 10 shows the relationship between the Business Process Model and the Decision Model.

1. The order is received and the customer is checked on the database
2. New customers are entered in the database
3. The customer is checked for credit worthiness using a business rule task notation (BPMN)
4. The DRD Decision Model describes the business rule task decision making
5. The DRD check customer credit is either an internal or external Decision Service
6. If the credit check is positive, the order is processed and conformation is sent to the customer
7. If the credit check is questionable, finance will advise whether to proceed with the order. If allowed to proceed, an order conformation is sent to the customer with a request for COD
8. If customer credit is negative, the order is not processed and an Unable to Complete Order is sent to the customer

Note

In figure 10 the business rule task notation (BPMN) could be substituted for a service task notation (BPMN).

Decision Model with a Decision Service

Figure 11 shows the relationship between the Business Process Model, the Decision Model and the Decision Service.

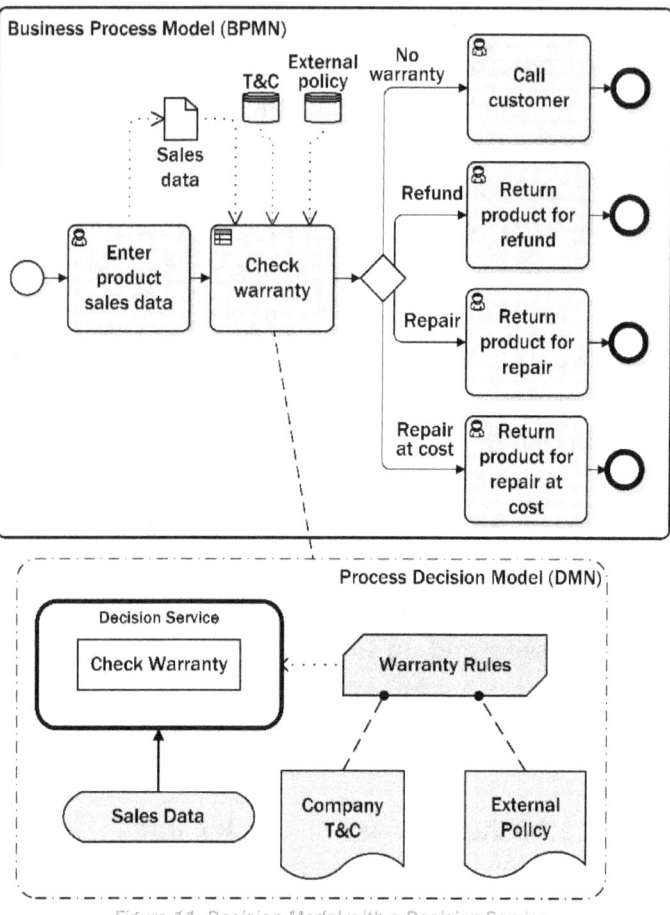

Figure 11: Decision Model with a Decision Service

DMN Pocket Reference

In figure 11

- The diagram depicts the business process of a product being returned either for refund or repair.
- The warranty business rules are checked against the sales date and current date.
- The sales information provided by the customer is the input data to the Decision Model.
- The information provided to the business knowledge model are
  1. Company terms and conditions
  2. External policy on product returns e.g. a product can be returned for repair within 6 years of purchase at cost to the customer.

The decision outcomes:
- Call customer
- Return product for refund
- Return product for repair
- Return product for repair at cost

NOTES

DMN Pocket Reference

Decision Requirements Graph

A Decision Requirements Graph (DRG) contains the decision-making elements and the dependencies of the decision requirements for a specific business scenario i.e. decisions, input data and knowledge sources.

A DRG is made up of elements connected by Requirements notations.

A DRG should contain all the modelled decision requirements necessary and can include more than one DRD.

Simply put

- A DRG represents a complete Decision Model with all the relevant decisions, data inputs and knowledge sources for a specific business decision scenario

- A DRG represents a specific view of a Decision Model which may be a partial or filtered display

DRG Example 1

Figure 12 shows a DRG business scenario called Select a Vacation.

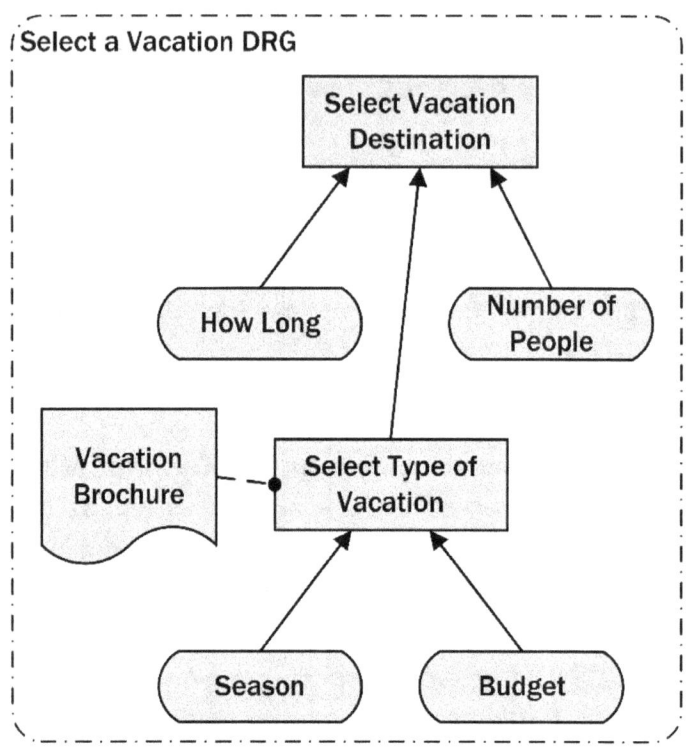

Figure 12: Select a vacation DRG

Example 1 description:

DRG Name: Select a vacation
Knowledge Source: Vacation Brochure
Input Data:
- Season
- Budget
- How Long
- Number of People

Decisions:
- Select Type of Vacation
- Select Vacation Destination

DRG Example 2

Figure 13 is a DRG scenario to purchase a printer from selected suppliers.

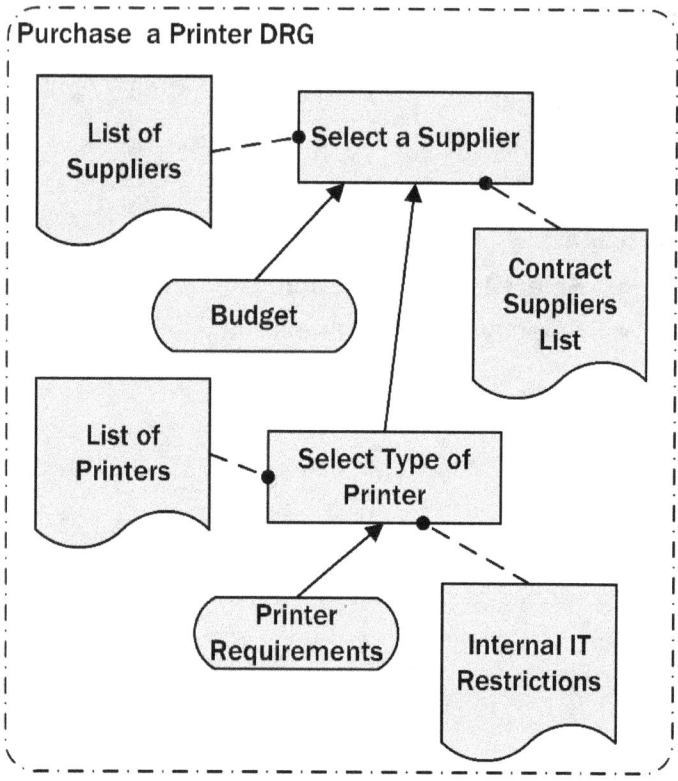

Figure 13: Purchase a printer DRG

Example 2 description

DRG Name: Purchase a printer
Knowledge Sources:

- List of printers
- Internal IT restrictions
- List of suppliers
- Contract suppliers list

Input Data:

- Printer requirements
- Budget

Decisions:

- Select type of printer
- Select a supplier

NOTES

Decision Logic Requirements

This section introduces the principles by which decision logic are associated with elements in a DRG and are expressed by the following

- Literal Expressions
- Decision Tables
- Invocations

Simply put

- A literal expression is an expression or equation in which the constants are represented by text

- A decision table is a tabular representation of a set of related input and output expressions organised into rules, indicating which output entry applies to a specific set of input entries

- An invocation is a binding expression of the decision table parameters which are contained in an invocation table

Literal Expression

A Literal Expression represents the output value which is derived from the input value, in text form.

Literal Expression examples

{age}
{age + 1}
{x * (y / z)}
{age GE 17}
{'a' IN name}

The above examples contain

- Variables (*age*, *name*, *x*, *y*, *z*)
- Numbers (1, 17)
- Arithmetical operators (+, *, /)
- A numerical comparison operator (GE) equates to (greater than or equal to)
- Literal text ('a')
- A string (text) comparison operator (IN) equates to (is contained in)

Decision Table

A method of describing the Decision Logic which is contained in a DRD Business Knowledge Model.

A Decision Table depicts rules arranged in table cells with inputs in the same order in every rule, making the table more legible and easier to verify.

A complete decision table contains all the possible input values required to determine the output.

Warranty Rules Example

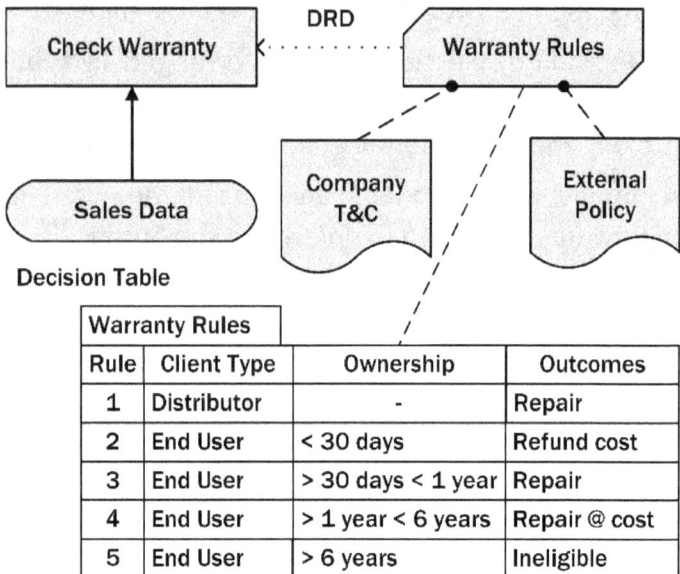

Decision Table

Warranty Rules			
Rule	Client Type	Ownership	Outcomes
1	Distributor	-	Repair
2	End User	< 30 days	Refund cost
3	End User	> 30 days < 1 year	Repair
4	End User	> 1 year < 6 years	Repair @ cost
5	End User	> 6 years	Ineligible

Figure 14: Warranty rules decision table

In figure 14

- Rule - refers to the warranty business rules
- Client Type - is obtained from the Sales Data
- Ownership - refers to a calculation of the sales date obtained from the Sales Data and current date
- Outcomes - refer to Check Warranty results

Invocation Table

An invocation is a Binding Expression of the decision table parameters contained in an Invocation Table.

The Invocation Table is a Boxed Expression and contains the explanation of each invocation.

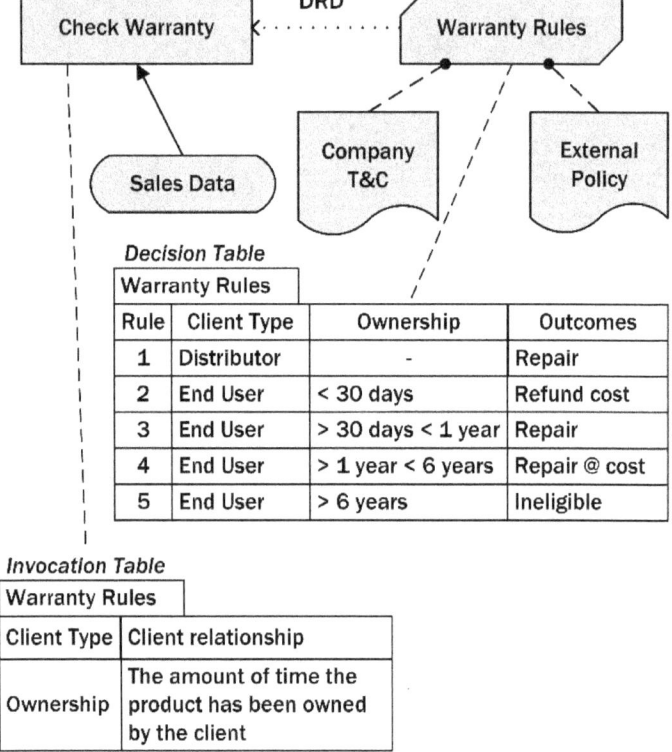

Figure 15: Warranty rules decision & Invocation tables

In figure 15

Client Type - is classed as an invocation and refers to the client relationship.

Ownership - is classed as an invocation and refers to the amount of time the product has been owned by the client.

The box on the left (Client Type) contains the name of a parameter and the box on the right (Client relationship) is a Binding Expression.

The Binding Expression is the value which is assigned to the parameter for the purpose of evaluating the business knowledge model.

Note

Both the Decision Table and the Invocation Table should be labelled with the same name to avoid confusion with other tables in a DRG.

NOTES

Boxed Expressions

A Boxed Expression is depicted as a graphical notation containing the Decision Logic in a table form.

A Boxed Expression notation serves to break down the Decision Logic Model into small parts that can be associated with other DRD notations.

The DRD including the Boxed Expression notations form a complete, although mostly graphical language, that encompasses DRG decision models.

Types of Boxed Expressions

There are two types of Boxed Expressions

- Literal
- Invocation

A Boxed Expression notation can be one of the following

- Decision table
- Invocation table
- FEEL expression
- A context
- A list
- A relation
- A function

Simply put

- A boxed literal expression is represented by text
- A boxed invocation expression describes the parameters being used and the binding expression to the decision logic
- Boxed Expressions can contain other boxed expressions
- The top-level Boxed Expression corresponds to the decision logic of a single DRG notation
- Boxed Expressions should have the same name as the DRG notation

Boxed Literal Expression

To improve the clarity of Boxed Literal Expressions there are two notational conventions

- String literals
- Date and time literals

Boxed Literal Expressions can be represented in two ways

- Italicised literals - Figure 16 the Risk Category column
- String literal - Figure 17 the Risk Category column

The Risk Category columns in Figures 16 and 17 in principle are the same expressions.

Credit Card Factor		
U	Risk Category	Credit Contingency Factor
1	*High, Very High*	80%
2	*Medium*	50%
3	*Low, Very Low*	20%

Figure 16: Decision table with italicised literals

Credit Card Factor		
U	Risk Category	Credit Contingency Factor
1	"High or Very High"	80%
2	"Medium"	50%
3	"Low or Very Low"	20%

Figure17: Decision table with string literals

Figure 16 shows the italicised literals with commas.

Figure 17 shows the string literals free of commas.

Note

Date and time string literals such as date "2013-08-09" can be alternatively represented by the italicized literal *2013-08-09*.

Boxed Invocation Expression

A Boxed Invocation Expression describes the parameters being used and the binding expression to the decision logic.

An invocation table describes the parameters and the bindings.

The binding expression is the value which is assigned to the parameter for the purpose of evaluating a Business Knowledge Model.

An Invocation Expression is shown as a two-boxed expression in a row.

In figure 18 the box on the left contains the name of the parameter and the box on the right contains the Binding Expression.

Name of the Business Knowledge Model	
Parameter 1	Binding expression 1
Parameter 2	Binding expression 2
Parameter 3	Binding expression 3
Parameter n	Binding expression n

Figure 18: Boxed invocation

Decision Tables

Decision Tables express the Decision Logic in language which corresponds to DRD Decision notations.

Decision Tables represent a set of related input and output expressions, organised into rules indicating which output entry applies to a specific set of input entries.

A complete Decision Table contains all possible combinations of input values and outcomes.

Decision Table Requirements

- The name of the decision or business knowledge model
- An output label in text form
- The outcome of a Decision Table must be referenced using the information item name
- Each table input consists of an input expression and a number of input entries
- A single Decision Table output requires a value only
- Two or more Decision Table outputs are called Output Components and are named separately
- Each Output Component should specify an output entry for each rule

- If the rules are expressed as rows, the columns are the Output Clauses
- If the rules are expressed as columns, the rows are the Output Clauses
- An Output Clause in a Decision Table refers to component names and all output entries
- The rules in rows or columns in the Decision Table are composed of the specific input and output entries

DMN Pocket Reference

Types of Decision Tables

- Crosstab: a classic Decision Table where each row and column represent a specific decision (not rule based)
- Vertical orientation: uses rules as columns and multiple output components
- Horizontal orientation: uses rules as rows and multiple output components

Crosstab Tables

A Crosstab table is a data table that displays the joint distribution of two or more variables simultaneously.

Sometimes called pivot tables, they make it easy to sort, count and total data.

Example of a Simple Crosstab Table

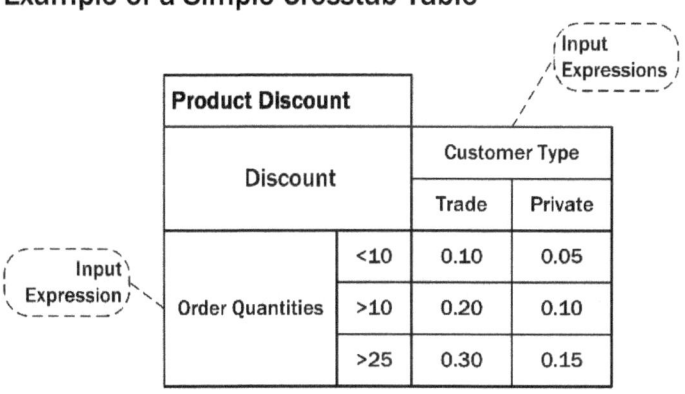

Figure 19 Simple Crosstab table

Hit Policy

A Decision Table normally has several rules and as a default rules do not overlap.

In cases of overlapping rules i.e. when more than one rule matches the input data, a hit policy is required.

The hit policy is an indicator used in order to recognize the table type and understand the decision logic.

The hit policy is defined as one of the following:

U = Unique

A = Any

P = Priority

F = First

C = Collect

O = Output order

R = Rule order

The hit policy character uses the initial letter of the hit policy

The hit policy is not used in crosstab tables

Tables with a Single Output Component

The following examples show a horizontal and a vertical table with the customer type and order quantities as input data.

The output decision is the discount value.

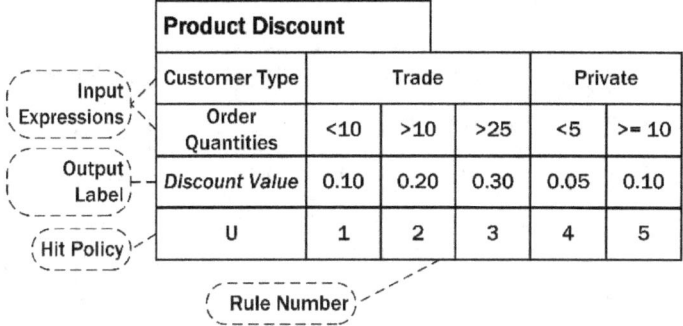

Figure 20: Vertical orientation with rules as columns

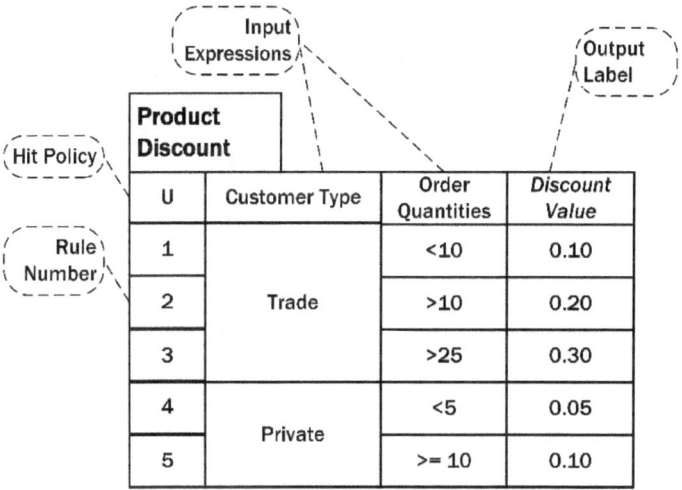

Figure 21: Horizontal orientation with rules as rows

Tables with Multiple Output Components

The following examples show the customer type and order quantities are the input data.

The discount value and delivery type are the output decisions.

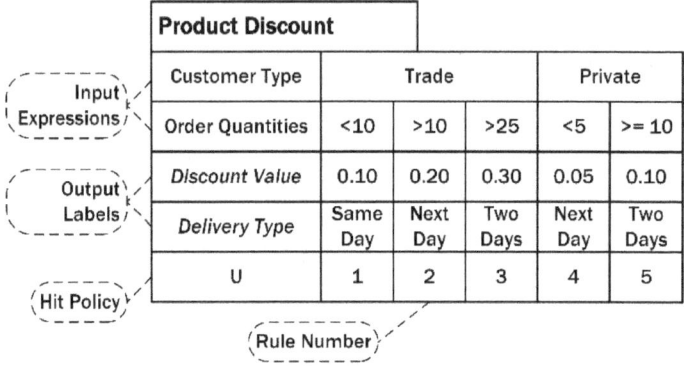

Product Discount					
Customer Type	Trade			Private	
Order Quantities	<10	>10	>25	<5	>= 10
Discount Value	0.10	0.20	0.30	0.05	0.10
Delivery Type	Same Day	Next Day	Two Days	Next Day	Two Days
U	1	2	3	4	5

Figure 22: Vertical orientation with multiple output components

Product Discount				
P	Customer Type	Order Quantities	*Discount Value*	*Delivery Type*
1	Trade	< 10	0.10	Same Day
2	Trade	> 10	0.20	Next Day
3	Trade	> 25	0.30	Two Days
4	Private	< 5	0.05	Next Day
5	Private	>= 10	0.10	Two Days

Figure 23: Horizontal orientation with multiple output components

DMN Decision Table Standards

- The orientation uses rules as rows, columns or crosstab
- Inputs, outputs and optional allowed values are placed in standard locations on a grid of cells
- Input expressions are optionally associated with unary tests restricting the allowed input values. In this context the optional cells with allowed values are indicated in inverse
- Output components are optionally associated with allowed values. In this context the optional allowed output values are indicated in inverse
- Optional use of line style and or colour
- The hit policy, indicating how to interpret overlapping input combinations
- Placement of information item name, hit policy and rule numbers
- Rule numbers are consecutive starting at 1
- Rule numbering is required for tables with hit indicator F (first) or R (rule order), because the meaning depends on the rule sequence
- Crosstab tables have no rule numbers
- Rule numbering is optional for other table types

NOTES

DMN Pocket Reference

Friendly Enough Expression Language (FEEL)

FEEL is a set of definitions of standard executable semantics for expressions in a Decision Model as defined in DMN specification 1.1.

FEEL is used in situations where the expressions can be used in specific program languages.

FEEL has two roles in DMN

1. As a Text notation in Boxed Expressions i.e. decision tables.
   Boxed Expressions used in Decision Tables are compatible with program languages.

2. Used to represent the logic of expressions by composing the semantics in a simple and uniform way.

Decision Boxed Expressions are FEEL expressions. with the following features

- Side-effect free
- Simple data model with numbers, dates, strings, lists, and contexts
- Simple syntax designed for a wide audience
- Three-valued logic (true, false, null) based on SQL and PMML

The FEEL Syntax Grammar Rules

1. expression =

1.a textual expression |

1.b boxed expression ;

2. textual expression =

2.a function definition | for expression | if expression | quantified expression |

2.b disjunction |

2.c conjunction |

2.d comparison |

2.e arithmetic expression |

2.f instance of |

2.g path expression |

2.h filter expression | function invocation |

2.i literal | simple positive unary test | name | "(" , textual expression , ")" ;

3. textual expressions = textual expression, { "," , textual expression } ;

4. arithmetic expression =

4.a addition | subtraction |

4.b multiplication | division |

4.c   exponentiation |

4.d   arithmetic negation ;

5.   simple expression = arithmetic expression | simple value;

6.   simple expressions = simple expression, {"," simple expression } ;

7.   simple positive unary test =

7.a   ["<" | "<=" | ">" | ">="] , endpoint |

7.b   interval ;

8.   interval = (open interval start | closed interval start) , endpoint , ".." , endpoint , (open interval end | closed interval end) ;

9.   open interval start = "(" | "]" ;

10.   closed interval start = "[" ;

11.   open interval end = ")" | "[" ;

12.   closed interval end = "]" ;

13.   simple positive unary tests = simple positive unary test, { "," , simple positive unary test } ;

14.   simple unary tests =

14.a   simple positive unary tests |

14.b   "not", "(", simple positive unary tests, ")" |

14.c   "-";

15.   positive unary test = simple positive unary
       test | "null" ;

16.   positive unary tests = positive unary test, {
       "," , positive unary test } ;

17.   unary tests =

17.a   positive unary tests |

17.b   "not", " (", positive unary tests, ")" |

17.c   "-"

18.   endpoint = simple value ;

19.   simple value = qualified name | simple
       literal ;

20.   qualified name = name , { "." , name } ;

21.   addition = expression , "+" , expression ;

22.   subtraction = expression , "-" , expression ;

23.   multiplication = expression , "*" ,
       expression ;

24.   division = expression , "/" , expression ;

25.   exponentiation = expression, "**",
       expression ;

26.   arithmetic negation = "-" , expression ;

27.   name = name start , { name part |
       additional name symbols } ;

28.   name start = name start char, { name part
       char } ;

29.   name part = name part char , { name part
       char } ;

30.   name start char = "?" | [A-Z] | "_" | [a-z] |
       [\uC0-\uD6] | [\uD8-\uF6] | [\uF8-\u2FF] |
       [\u370-\u37D] | [\u37F-\u1FFF] |
       [\u200C-\u200D] | [\u2070-\u218F] |
       [\u2C00-\u2FEF] | [\u3001-\uD7FF] |
       [\uF900-\uFDCF] | [\uFDF0-\uFFFD] |
       [\u10000-\uEFFFF] ;

31.   name part char = name start char | digit |
       \uB7 | [\u0300-\u036F] | [\u203F-
       \u2040] ;

32.   additional name symbols = "." | "/" | "-" |
       "'" | "+" | "*" ;

33.   literal = simple literal | "null" ;

34.   simple literal = numeric literal | string
       literal | Boolean literal | date time literal ;

35.   string literal = "" , { character – ("" | vertical
       space) }, "" ;

36.   Boolean literal = "true" | "false" ;

37.   numeric literal = ["-"] , (digits , [".", digits]
       | "." , digits) ;

38.   digit = [0-9] ;

39.   digits = digit , {digit} ;

40.   function invocation = expression , parameters ;

41.   parameters = "(" , (named parameters | positional parameters) , ")" ;

42.   named parameters = parameter name , ":" , expression , { "," , parameter name , ":" , expression } ;

43.   parameter name = name ;

44.   positional parameters = [expression , { "," , expression }] ;

45.   path expression = expression , "." , name ;

46.   for expression = "for" , name , "in" , expression { "," , name , "in" , expression } , "return" , expression ;

47.   if expression = "if" , expression , "then" , expression , "else" expression ;

48.   quantified expression = ("some" | "every") , name , "in" , expression , { name , "in" , expression } , "satisfies" , expression ;

49.   disjunction = expression , "or" , expression ;

50.   conjunction = expression , "and" , expression ;

51. comparison =

51.a expression , ("=" | "!=" | "<" | "<=" | ">" | ">=") , expression |

51.b expression , "between" , expression , "and" , expression |

51.c expression , "in" , positive unary test ;

51.d expression , "in" , " (", positive unary tests, ")" ;

52. filter expression = expression , "[" , expression , "]" ;

53. instance of = expression , "instance" , "of" , type ;

54. type = qualified name ;

55. boxed expression = list | function definition | context ;

56. list = "[" [expression , { "," , expression }] , "]" ;

57. function definition = "function" , "(" , [formal parameter { "," , formal parameter }] , ")" , ["external"] , expression ;

58. formal parameter = parameter name ;

59. context = "{" , [context entry , { "," , context entry }] , "}" ;

60. context entry = key , ":" , expression ;

61.   key = name | string literal ;

62.   date time literal = ("date" | "time" | "date
       and time" | "duration") , "(" , string literal ,
       ")" ;

Additional Syntax Rules

In grammar rules 1, 2 and 4, order Operator
precedence is given by order of alternatives, from
lowest to highest.

- Boxed Invocation has higher precedence than
  multiplication
- Multiplication has higher precedence than
  addition
- Addition has higher precedence than
  comparison
- Addition and subtraction have equal precedence
- A name may contain spaces but may not contain
  a sequence of 2 or more spaces
- A name start (grammar rule 28) will not be a
  language keyword. (Language keywords are
  enclosed in double quotes in the grammar rules,
  for example, "and", "or", "true", "false".)
- A name part (grammar rule 29) can be a
  language keyword
- Java-style comments can be used, i.e. '//' to end
  of line and /* ... */

Notation Summary

DRD Notations

Decision	Notation
A Decision notation represents the decision logic output produced from a number of inputs, which may be referenced by one or more Business Knowledge Model notations.	Decision
Business Knowledge Model	Notation
The Business Knowledge Model represents a function which concentrates business knowledge for a process decision.	Business Knowledge Model

Input Data	Notation
An Input Data notation represents the active information provided by the business process requirements.	Input Data
Listed Input Data	Notation
The Listed Input Data notation is an alternative way to display requirements for input data combined with a decision notation.	Decision Data Input 1 Data Input 2
Knowledge Source	Notation
The Knowledge Source notation represents the information derived from an authoritative source.	Knowledge Source

Artefacts Summary

Text Annotation	Notation
A Text Annotation notation is a mechanism for modellers to provide additional text information.	Text Annotation
Association	Notation
An Association notation connector links a Text Annotation to DRD elements.	· · · · · · · · · · Association · · · · · · · · · ·
Group	Notation
A Group notation is used to describe groups of decisions, business knowledge models, knowledge sources and input data notations, which are part of the same scenario.	Group

Decision Service Summary

Decision Service	Notation
A Decision Service notation shows a specific automated step in the business process sequence.	Decision Service Notation
Divided Decision Service	Notation
A Divided Decision Service notation is used if the decision requires two or more decision services as input to the decision logic.	Divided Decision Service Notation

DMN Pocket Reference

DRD Requirements Summary

Information Requirement	Notation
An Information Requirement notation shows input data or a decision output used as decision notatation input	Information Requirement ──────────▶
Knowledge Requirement	Notation
The Knowledge Requirement notation is used to show from where the specific static business knowledge is derived	Knowledge Requirement - - - - - -⟩
Authority Requirement	Notation
Authority Requirement notation Shows the dependence of a DRD notation on another DRD notation that acts as a source of guidance or knowledge	Authority Requirement - - - - ●

Requirements Connection Rules

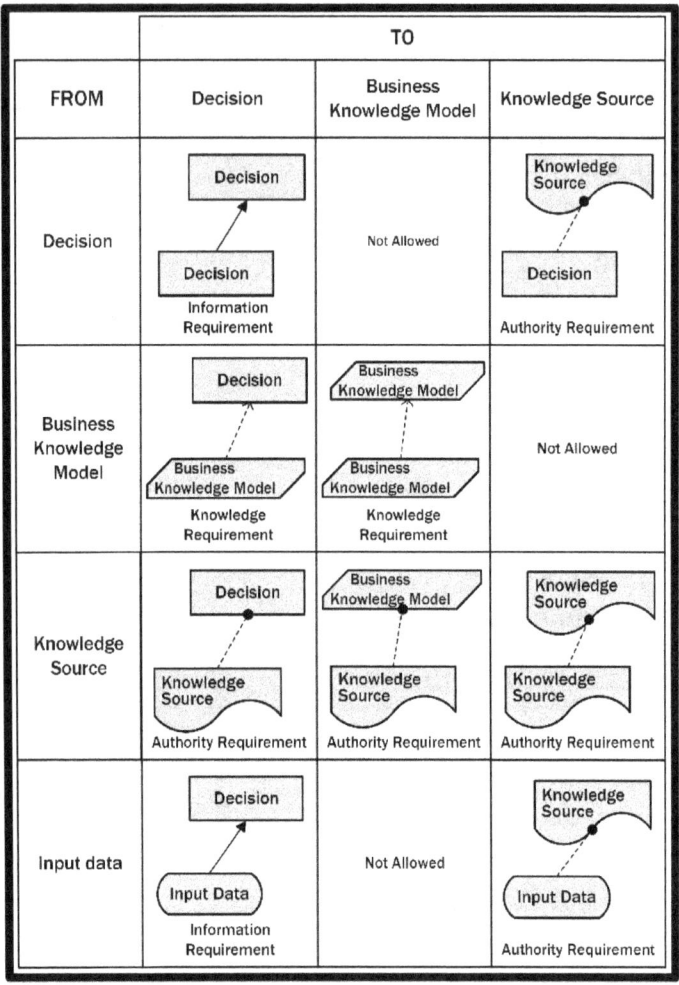

FROM	Decision	Business Knowledge Model	Knowledge Source
		TO	

Glossary

A

Any

> A hit policy for single hit decision tables with overlapping decision rules. Under this policy any match may be used.

Authority Requirement

> Shows the dependency of one element of a decision requirements graph on another element and provides guidance or acts as a source of knowledge.

B

Binding Expression

> A binding expression is a part of an invocation table associate with the decision table parameters.

Boxed Expression

> A notation used to break down the decision logic into small pieces which may be associated graphically with elements of a DRD.

Boxed Invocation

> A form of boxed expression showing the parameter bindings.

Boxed Literal Expression

A boxed literal expression is represented by a text.

Business Knowledge Model

Represents the required business knowledge for a specific decision process sequence task.

Business Rule

A business rule is a statement that defines what, how and when some aspects of the business are fulfilled.

A business rule is intended to assert business structure, to control, or influence the behaviour of a company.

Business Rule Decision Logic

The business rules used by the decision logic are derived from a business knowledge model.

C

Collect

A hit policy for multiple hit decision tables with overlapping decision rules.

Crosstab Table

An orientation for decision tables in which two input expressions form the two dimensions of the table, and the output entries form a two-dimensional grid.

D

Decision

> The act of determining an output value from a number of input values, using decision logic.

Decision Logic

> The logic used to make decisions, defined in DMN as the value expressions of decisions and business knowledge models and represented visually as boxed expressions.

Decision Logic Level

> The detailed level of modelling in DMN, consisting of the value expressions associated with decisions and business knowledge models.

Decision Model

> A formal model of an area of decision-making, expressed in DMN by decision requirements and decision logic.

Decision Point

> A point in a business process at which decision-making occurs, modelled in BPMN 2.0 as a business rule task and possibly implemented as a call to a decision service.

Decision Requirements Diagram

> A diagram presenting a view of a DRG.

Decision Requirements Graph

A graph of DRD notations, decisions, business knowledge models and input data, connected by requirements.

Decision Requirements Level

An abstract level of modelling in DMN, consisting of a DRG represented by one or more DRDs.

Decision Rule

In a decision table, a decision rule specifies a set of conditions.

Decision Service

A decision service is a specific automated process decision task and has a set of predetermined business rules.

Decision Table

A table representing a set of related input and output expressions organised into decision rules, indicating which output entry applies to a specific set of input entries.

DMN Element

Any element of a DMN decision model: a DRG Element, Business Context Element, Expression, Definitions, Element Collection, Information Item or Item Definition.

DRD

See decision requirements diagram.

DRG

See decision requirements graph.

DRG Element

Any component of a DRG: decision, business knowledge model, input data or knowledge source.

E

Expression

A literal, decision table or invocation expression used to define part of the decision logic for a decision model in DMN.

External Policy

Is a policy that is a system of principles to guide decisions and achieve rational outcomes created by an external organisation.

F

FEEL

The "Friendly Enough Expression Language" which is the default expression language for DMN.

First

> A hit policy for single hit decision tables with overlapping decision rules.
>
> With this policy the first match is used, based on the order of the decision rules.

G

Graphical Notation

> A graphical notation is a visual expression used in a DRG with defined graphical elements and boxed expressions.

H

Hit

> In a decision table, the successful matching of all input expressions of a decision rule, making the conclusion eligible for inclusion in the results.

Hit Policy

Indicates how overlapping decision rules have to be interpreted.

A single hit table returns the output of one rule only.

A multiple hit table may return the output of multiple rules or an aggregation of the outputs.

Horizontal

An orientation for decision tables in which decision rules are presented as rows; clauses as columns.

I

Information Requirement

The dependency of a decision on an input data element or another decision, to provide a variable used in decision logic.

Input Data

Denotes information used as an input by one or more decisions, whose value is defined outside the decision model.

Input Expression

An expression defining the item to be compared with the input entries of an input clause, in a decision table.

Input Value

An expression defining a limited range of expected values for an input clause in a decision table.

Invocation

An invocation is a binding expression of a decision table parameter and contained in an invocation table

Invocation Table

An invocation table is a boxed expression and contains the explanation of each invocation.

K

Knowledge Requirement

The dependency of a decision on a business knowledge model.

Knowledge Source

Information provided for decisions or business knowledge models, a company policy, the company warrantee Terms and Conditions or the company procurement policy etc.

L

Literal Expression

Text that represents decision logic by describing how an output value is derived from its input values, e.g. in plain English or using the default expression language FEEL.

M

Multiple Hit

A type of decision table which may return output entries from multiple decision rules.

O

Orientation

The style of presentation of a decision table.

Horizontal rules as rows, clauses as columns.

Vertical rules as columns, clauses as rows.

Crosstab rules composed of two input dimensions.

Output Clause

An output clause in a decision table refers to component names and all output entries.

If the rules are expressed as rows, the columns are the output clauses.

If the rules are expressed as columns, the rows are the output clauses.

Output Entry

An expression defining a conclusion cell in a decision table i.e. the intersection of a decision rule and an output clause.

Output Order

A hit policy for multiple hit decision tables with overlapping decision rules.

Using this policy all matches will be returned as a list in decreasing priority order.

Output priorities are specified in an ordered list of values.

Output Value

An expression defining a limited range of domain values for an output clause in a decision table.

P

Performance Indicator

A business context element representing a measure of business performance impacted by a decision.

Priority

A hit policy for single hit decision tables with overlapping decision rules.

Using this policy, the match is used that has the highest output priority.

Output priorities are specified in an ordered list of values.

R

Requirement

The dependency of one DRD element on another.

Rule Order

A hit policy for multiple hit decision tables with overlapping decisions.

Rules under this policy all matches will be returned as a list in the order of definition of the decision rules.

Rules

See business rules

S

Single Hit

A decision table which can return the output entry of only a single decision rule.

U

Unique

> A hit policy for single hit decision tables in which no overlap is possible and all decision rules are exclusive.

V

Variable

> Represents a value that is an input to a decision logic.

Vertical

> An orientation for decision tables in which rules are presented as columns and clauses as rows.

Further Books by the Author

BPMN Process Examples

ISBN-13 978-1515353935

The aim of this book is to demonstrate the practical use of BPMN in modelling business processes.

The book comprises of six complete examples of end to end business process models which come from operational business processes.

Each example has an overview, the choreography between the collaborating partners and the BPD of the inline sub-processes.

In each example the sub-process BPD's depict the tasks needed to complete the inline process.

The book pages are so designed that the description is on the left side of the page and the BPD on the right, allowing the reader to view the description and the BPD at the same time.

Business Process Collaboration

ISBN-13 978-1494400217

Business Process Collaboration is a course book specifically written for those who are interested in extending their knowledge of business process modelling.

This book assumes the reader has a basic knowledge of business process modelling using BPMN specification version 2.0.

The BPMN latest version 2.0.1 released September 2013 has been taken into account.

This course book includes diagrams, descriptions and covers all aspects of business process collaboration.

It also includes question time and student exercises with answers.

Test Your BPMN

ISBN-13 978-1519792136

Test Your BPMN has been written specifically for users of Business Processes.

This book tests their knowledge and understanding of the BPMN 2.02 specification and can be used as part of the preparation for a certification exam.

Test Your BPMN consists of 50 multiple choice questions which challenge the reader on their knowledge of the notations.

Test Your BPMN also contains 15 multiple choice questions using BPMN diagrams requiring the reader to investigate the incorrect notations.
Answers with detailed explanations can be found at the end of the book, allowing the reader to complete the test and then check the answers.

Test Your BPMN can be used in conjunction with Business Process Modelling with BPMN course book and the Complete BPMN Pocket Reference

www.admaks.com

kenneth@admaks.com